The Surgeon

Contents

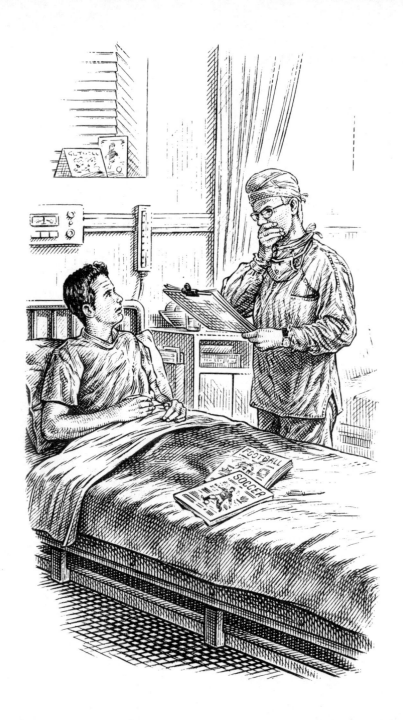

ER/ROB

A MEMBER OF THE HODDER HEADLINE GROUP

Acknowledgements
Cover: Dave Smith
Illustrations: Dave Hopkins

Orders: please contact Bookpoint Ltd, 78 Milton Park, Abingdon, Oxon OX14 4TD. Telephone: (44) 01235 827720, Fax: (44) 01235 400454. Lines are open from 9.00 – 6.00, Monday to Saturday, with a 24 hour message answering service. Email address: orders@bookpoint.co.uk

British Library Cataloguing in Publication Data
A catalogue record for this title is available from The British Library

ISBN 0 340 80055 0

First published 2001
Impression number   10 9 8 7 6 5 4 3 2 1
Year   2007 2006 2005 2004 2003 2002 2001

Copyright © 2001 Brandon Robshaw

Typeset by SX Composing DTP, Rayleigh, Essex.
Printed in Great Britain for Hodder & Stoughton Educational, a division of Hodder Headline Plc, 338 Euston Road, London NW1 3BH, by Athenaeum Press, Gateshead, Tyne & Wear.

1

Bad News

'I'm afraid I have some bad news for you,'
said the surgeon.
Ken looked up at the surgeon,
standing by the bed.
Dr Lewis, his name was.
He looked very serious.

'What's the matter?' asked Ken.
The last thing he remembered
was being wheeled into the operation theatre.
'The operation – did it go all right?'

'Well – not exactly,' said the surgeon.
He looked very unhappy.

'Come on, doctor –
it was only a minor op!
What could have gone wrong?'

Ken had gone in to have an
ingrowing toenail fixed.
It was only a small operation.
But the toe had been hurting him quite badly.
It was stopping him playing football.

'What's the matter?' asked Ken.
'Didn't you remove the toenail?'

Dr Lewis coughed.
'Oh yes, we removed it,' he said.

'Then what's the problem?' asked Ken.

'Well . . .' said the surgeon.
He seemed lost for words.
'There was – a mistake.'

'Come on!' said Ken.
'Just tell me what's happened!
I can take it.'

'Well . . .' said Dr Lewis.
'There was a mix-up.
Your chart got mixed up with
another patient's.
And that patient needed
to have both legs amputated.'

Ken stared at him.
'What do you mean?
You're not saying . . .?'

'I'm very, very sorry indeed,' said Dr Lewis.
'But – we've amputated both your legs.'

Ken threw back the bedclothes.
He saw the legs of his pyjamas
lying flat and empty on the bed.

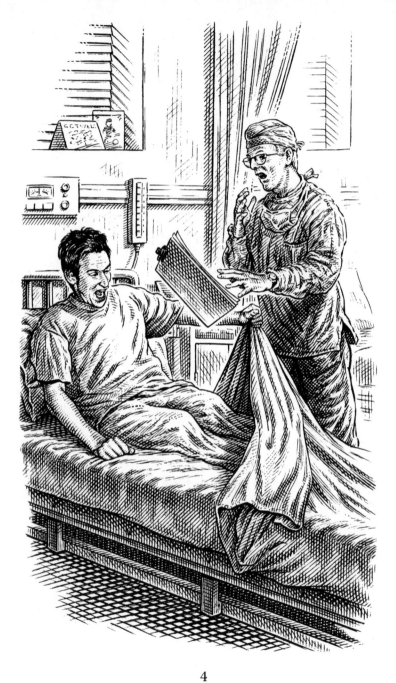

2

'I'll get you for this!'

Ken screamed.
He went on screaming.

'Please . . .' said Dr Lewis.
'Calm down.
It was a tragic mistake.
But you'll get compensation . . .'

'Compensation!' screamed Ken.
'How can you compensate me for this?
I was going to be a footballer –
did you know that?
I had a trial for West Ham coming up.
How are you going to compensate me
for that?
Get me a new pair of legs?'

He was shouting so loudly
that everyone in the ward was turning to look.
Two nurses came running down the ward.

'You need to sleep,' said Dr Lewis.
'We'll talk when you're calmer.'

'I'll get you for this, Lewis!' screamed Ken.
'I will – I'll get you for this!'

One of the nurses held Ken's arm.
The other stuck a needle in.

'I'll get you for this,' said Ken, more quietly.
Then the drug took effect.
He closed his eyes.
He was asleep.

Dr Lewis turned and walked away
from the bed.
He was shaking.

3

New Legs

The hospital gave Ken a pair of artificial legs.
They were made of pink plastic.
They strapped on to the stumps of his thighs.

Ken stayed in hospital
while he learned to use the new legs.
Doctors worked with him,
helping him, training him.
Not Dr Lewis, though.
Ken wouldn't let Lewis anywhere near him.

Walking with the new legs was difficult.
It was like walking on stilts.
It took Ken a few weeks before
he could get around in them.
Even then he was a bit unsteady.
He couldn't walk far without getting tired.
He'd never play football again,
that was for sure.

He could only walk short distances.
He'd need a wheelchair most of the time.
The hospital gave him one.
They said it was time for him to go home.

On the day Ken was going home,
there was a tap at his door.
Ken walked over on his plastic legs.
He opened the door.
Dr Lewis was standing there.

'You!' said Ken.
'What do you want?'

'Can I come in?' asked Dr Lewis.

'No,' said Ken.

'All right,' said Dr Lewis.
'I just came to – to wish you luck.'

Ken laughed. 'That's great!
He cuts off my legs, then he wishes me luck!'

'About your compensation,' said Dr Lewis.
'The hospital accepts that we were at fault.
We're offering you a million pounds.'

'A million pounds.
That won't bring me my legs back, will it?'

'No,' said Dr Lewis.
'I can't tell you how badly I feel about this.'

'You feel badly!
That's a good one.
So what are you saying –
I'm supposed to feel sorry for you?'

'No, no,' said Dr Lewis.
'I just wanted you to know how sorry I am.'

'You're going to be a damned sight sorrier,
Lewis,' said Ken.
'I'm going to get you.
I told you that before,
and I meant it.'

Then he closed the door in Dr Lewis's face.

4

The Letter

Dr Lewis watched from the window
as a nurse wheeled Ken towards
a waiting ambulance.
The ambulance door opened.
The nurse wheeled Ken inside.
The door closed.
The ambulance drove away.

Dr Lewis sighed with relief.
He felt bad about what had happened.
But he was glad Ken had gone now.

He looked at his watch.
Plenty of time.
Nothing on his list until the afternoon.
He went to the canteen to get a cup of coffee.

In the canteen, he saw Sarah Davey.
She was a surgeon too.
'Hi,' she said.
'Come and sit with me.
How are you feeling?'

'Bad,' said Dr Lewis. 'But a bit better now
he's gone.'

'You've got to stop worrying about it,'
said Sarah.
'It was an accident.
We all make mistakes.
I've made them.'

'Yes, but not as bad as that.'

'No, not as bad as that,' said Sarah.
'It was a terrible accident.
However, you mustn't let it wreck your life.
You're a good surgeon.
Anyone who's worked with you
knows that.'

'Yes. I suppose you're right,' said Dr Lewis.
He sipped his coffee.

'He's got his compensation now
and he'll have to get on with his life.
And you'll have to get on with yours.
It's over now.'

'Yes,' said Dr Lewis.
'It's over.'

Or was it over?
The next day Dr Lewis got a letter.
There was just one sentence.
'I'M GOING TO OPERATE ON YOU,'
it said.

It wasn't signed.
But Dr Lewis had a pretty good idea
who it was from.

5

A Nasty Surprise

He showed the letter to Sarah.
'What do you think?'

Sarah looked at it.
'From Ken, of course.'

'Of course.
What do you think I should do?
Call the police?'

'No, no, no.
Forget it.
The guy won't do anything.
He's feeling angry and bitter.
Well, you can understand that.
The best thing is just to wait
and let him get over it.'

'Are you sure?'

'Sure I'm sure.
If you react, he may carry on.
If you ignore it,
he'll give up.
He'll get on with his life.'

Dr Lewis took Sarah's advice.
He ignored the letter.
It looked as if Sarah was right,
because he didn't hear from Ken again.

A few weeks went by
and Dr Lewis began to feel easier.
He stopped worrying about Ken.
It was all over now.

Then, one night, he got a nasty surprise.

He had finished work late.
There were only a few cars left
in the car park by the time
he came out.
As he walked towards his car,
a figure loomed up out of the dark.
The figure walked towards him,
stiffly and slowly.
It was Ken.

'Evening, Lewis,' said Ken.

Dr Lewis forced himself to keep calm.
'Good evening, Ken.
How are you?'

Ken laughed.
'You're amazing, Lewis, you know that?
You cut my legs off
and then ask me how I am.'
He stopped laughing.
'Is this your car?'

Dr Lewis nodded.

'Get in,' said Ken.
'We're going for a little ride.'

'Now look,' said Dr Lewis.
'I don't know what you're playing at, but –'
Ken reached into his pocket.
He took out a gun.
He pointed it at Lewis's face.

'Get in,' he said again.
'We're going for a ride.'

6

A Blow on the Head

They drove through the dark streets.
'Nice car,' said Ken.
'You must be doing well to afford
a car like this.'

Dr Lewis didn't say anything.

'Listen,' said Dr Lewis,
'I'm very, very sorry for what happened –
but this is no way to . . .'

'Shut up, Lewis,' said Ken.
'Turn right here.
OK, next left.
Right, pull up just here.'

They stopped in a quiet street
outside a large, dark house.
'This is my house,' said Ken.
'Do you like it?
I bought it with the compensation.'

'It's very nice,' said Dr Lewis.
'Now, I really must be getting home.'

Ken pointed the gun at his face again.
'Not yet, Lewis.
I'm inviting you into my house.
You'd better not refuse.
That would be rude.
It would make me angry.'

Dr Lewis looked at the gun.
He'd better do as Ken said.
'All right,' he said.
'I'll come in for a little while.'

They got out of the car
and walked up the path.
Ken opened the door. 'In you go, Lewis.'

Dr Lewis stepped into the dark hall.
He'd only gone a few steps
when he felt a stunning blow on the head.
He saw a crowd of bright stars
and then everything went black.

7

The Operating Theatre

When Dr Lewis woke up,
he didn't know where he was at first.
He was staring up at the ceiling.
There was a bright light above.
He tried to get up, but he couldn't move.
He was strapped down.
Strapped to a bed.

'Where am I?' he said.

'Oh, good, you're awake,' said a voice.
It was Ken.
'You're in my operating theatre.
What do you think of it?'

Dr Lewis looked around.
The room did look like an operating theatre.
The bright light,
the bed he was strapped to,
the bare walls.
There was a metal sink,
and a trolley full of glittering
metal instruments.

'If this is a joke,' said Dr Lewis,
'it's gone far enough.
You'd better let me go or . . .'

'But it's not a joke, Lewis,' said Ken.
He stepped into view.
He was wearing a green gown
and a green mask over his mouth.
He went over to the sink
and began to wash his hands.
'It's not a joke at all.'

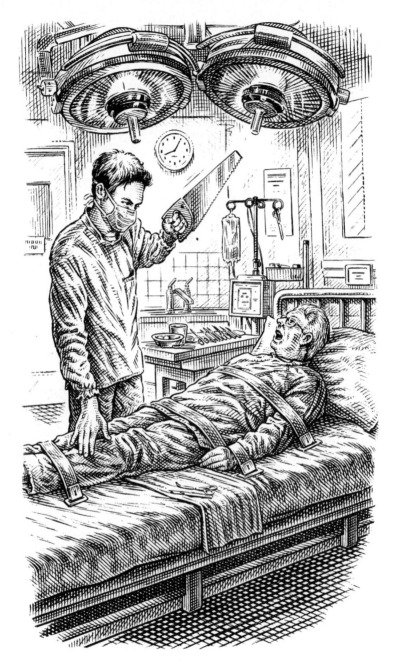

8

The Operation

'I spent the rest of the compensation money
getting this room turned into
an operating theatre,' said Ken.
'What do you think?
It's good, isn't it?
The walls are soundproofed, by the way,
so it's no good screaming.
But I expect you will anyway.'

'Please,' said Dr Lewis.
'Whatever you're thinking of doing –
don't do it.'

'That's a good line,' said Ken.
'I wish somebody had said it to you
before my operation.'

He put on a pair of rubber gloves.
He walked stiffly over to the
instrument trolley.
Then he walked back towards the bed.
He was holding a saw.

'Please,' said Dr Lewis.

'I'm afraid I haven't got any anaesthetic,'
said Ken.
'So this may hurt a little.'